teeming

Praise for *Teething*

'Both fluent and complex, searing and plangent, the poems in Megha Rao's *Teething* reveal a remarkable sensibility allied to a rare talent for the language. This is a stunning, moving collection. I look forward to many more!'

—*Dr Shashi Tharoor*

'If poetry is a metaphorical description of the mundane then Megha Rao is certainly not short of metaphors. These deeply-felt personal poems sometimes have the touch of a butterfly's wings and sometimes hit the reader like a sledgehammer.'

—*Naseeruddin Shah*

'Megha Rao breaks new ground with her poetry, effortlessly spanning the intimate and the desolate, beedis and beef biriyani, confessions and love letters. This is a collection at once bold and quiet, a study in love and loss and the yearning for those secret gardens we have all lost.'

—*Jerry Pinto*

'The poems in Megha Rao's *Teething* are jagged and sweet. They shift between survival and heartbreak, the street and the hearth. They wear pearls in the dark.'

—*Tishani* Doshi

'Devastatingly sharp, with few layers left unpeeled, each line in Megha Rao's poetry holds up a mirror. There is the ugly, and there is the profound. There is the human, and there is something that lies beyond. Above all, there is honesty and a strength of reflection, sending many a chill down the spine. And yet, every now and then, there is also a glow of memory and warmth; through every loss, also a fight to live on.'

—*Manu S Pillai*

teething

Megha Rao

HarperCollins *Publishers* India

First published in India by
HarperCollins *Publishers* in 2022
Building No 10, Tower A, 4th Floor,
DLF Cyber City, Phase II, Gurugram 122002
www.harpercollins.co.in

2 4 6 8 10 9 7 5 3 1

P-ISBN: 978-93-5489-430-5
E-ISBN: 978-93-5489-434-3

Cover design: Amit Malhotra
Cover art: Shakil Solanki

Typeset in 11.5/15.5 Minion Pro at
Manipal Digital Systems, Manipal

Printed and bound at
Thomson Press (India) Ltd

🅕🅘🅞🅞HarperCollinsIn

For Stuti

Contents

A Love Like Mollywood

Letters to Home

Foreword

Teething reads like a memoir. Megha begins the book with the story of her birth and you're immediately drawn into her life. You watch her step into this life through her mother. She ends the book with a confession and you watch her step out with her mother.

The first time I saw Megha, she was the loudest thing in the room despite standing in the corner quietly—her hair chopped into an aesthetic shag, painted bright blue, pitch black kohl on her eyes, going perfectly well with the choker on her neck and the silver ring pierced in her septum. I couldn't take my eyes off her. I was part curious, part in awe. In an interview she says, she creates 'art for life's sake', that her work is a reflection of who she is and where she is at the moment. Over the years, as I've followed her work and transitions, I've come to understand that her creative expression bleeds through the pages of her notebooks—it's on her body reflected in tattoos, painted art, piercings and measured in the depth and exaggeration of her kohl. It's difficult not to be pulled into Megha's world, both in life and on paper in this book.

To me all art is about love. It's about the absence of love, the presence of love, the inability of love, the various versions of love and the negotiations of love. But how do we as young women understand love? Where do we learn it from? In her remarkable collection of poetry about three children from Kerala, Megha explores home, identity, community, trauma, politics to seek and answer those questions. The collection is split into three haunting chapters—in Second-hand Children, you find innocence and playfulness. A Love Like Mollywood is a dramatic, coming-of-age era. And finally, Letters to Home sheds all panic and mania, and settles into quiet acceptance.

Teething is a heartbreaking yet euphoric voyage, and Megha is unafraid to be vulnerable to life's violences as she continues to carry the trauma with force and pliability— letting us know that there is no other way for it to be.

Gurmehar Kaur

Prologue

My English teacher once told me you should never start a sentence with the word *because*. So I never told her that if there was one word to summarize my entire life, it was this.

You see, I was born with excuses in my mouth. *Why're you still alive?*

Because my mother's Church taught me that suicide was a sin.

Because it was the first thing Baba told me when he found the bottle of sleeping pills on the table I lay next to, my breath quietening underneath my ribs:

The Prophet said, 'whoever commits suicide with piece of iron will be punished with the same piece of iron in the Hell Fire.'

Because my sister and I couldn't get past the third sentence of our brother's suicide note or the way he giggled the day before, as his bunny teeth pressed over his lower lip in an effort to stop.

You see, *because* was a defensive word. A justification. An apology. *Why is your face always puffy?* Because I was crying. *Why were you crying?* Because a month after my brother died, my boyfriend left. *Why did he leave?* Because I was always sad. Because I saw him look at that girl in the Xerox shop. Because it's my fault I didn't have a body like that. *Why don't you have a body like that?* Because my relationship with my blade was bigger than my relationship with him.

Because the cuts got in the way and he didn't think I was beautiful anymore. *Why did you cut?* Because my past was after me and the blood distracted it. Because the biggest thing life stole from me was innocence, and I never saw the world the same way again.

Because it *hurts*.

And why does it hurt? Because we asked for balloons and got trauma instead. Because my sister saw things that made her wish she wasn't so young. Because the night we ran away from home, we felt guilt wash over our heads like the Johnson's baby shampoo our Mama had sold her silk sarees to buy. Because we couldn't save her.

Because there are days when I stand in front of her grave with freshly picked white carnation and think about how she wasted her love on us. Because there are days when I cry in front of her grave with excuses so loud for not loving her back.

Because, because, because. *Because.*

Because I still can't bring myself to ask my mother
if the collateral damage was
the stretch marks, or the *children*.

Second-hand Children

The Story of My Birth

If I am allowed one memory in the last days of my life,
then, God, let it be this:

Take me back to the very beginning of me,
when a passer-by was driven wild
by the ancient poetry of a woman's anklets in the rain,
and asked for her hand in marriage.

Back when I remembered my birth
as a moment in transcendental history,
unsullied by the heartache of growing up.

Sometimes I still climb up my terrace to the stars,
just to wonder about the wisdom of light years.

And if I am lucky,
somewhere in a bygone strand of time
a baby turns inside a womb,
sweetened by the symphony
of her father's love letters
to her mother.

Coconut Oil for Trauma Wounds

We brought things back from class.
The blood in my underwear.
The hickeys on my brother's neck.
A big F on my sister's report card
and her bruises from the bigger girls.
Our mother couldn't fix us,
but God, she tried to make us beautiful.
So she'd slip us into our uniforms
and spray him with cologne
and us, with perfume.
On the days we made it to school,
we smelled like dead flowers.
Things that happy graves were made of,
if someone loved them enough.

Susamma's Wine Shop

He still takes up only one side of the bed.
He still brings back her favourite drink
from Susamma's wine shop.
He still leaves half of his biscuit on her old desk.

Somewhere in Heaven
our grandmother eats
the rest of the Parle-G
with her false teeth.

Chocolates from the Gulf

When Sunny kochachan from Dubai arrives home,
he tells our father: *Chetta, take chechi to the cinema*
she needs a break from these kids.

And when my siblings are asleep,
Sunny kochachan strips his U.S. Polo stretched elastic briefs
and crowds my tiny hands with them, wheezing:

every time I give you something,
you say—thank you, darling.

Last evening, he was back again after three years of
        travelling the world.
He sits in the hall with our family discussing oil prices and
        Namboodiripad's Communist government.
I have some chocolates for you kids, he rasps. *From the Gulf.*

Before I can go get them,
my little sister's hand reaches out.
'Thank you, *darling*,' she says to Sunny kochachan
        innocently.

Second-hand Children

Life is a riddle, and waking up is the answer. It's the kind of night when fireflies eclipse the stars, and my baby sister's silhouette swallows my doorway as she shows up with her pillow and bedsheet. 'I can't sleep,' she whispers. 'Neither can I, Mol.' I pack Mama's homemade jackfruit jam, our midnight snack, and help her out of the window as we begin running, barefoot. We're sprinting like two magnificent wolves, howling our chests out, our silver anklets whistling violently as the wind begins a sultry affair with our hair. We're wild things no past can own, chasing dragonflies into the humid dark. We only stop at the beach to buy cheap devil-light crowns, and then race each other again, our heads flashing red, our horns locking, high-pitched laughter shooting into the air like fireworks during the Thrissur Pooram festival. Around us are strangers selling ripe golden mangoes and water guns, watching the rain fall on our faces, splattering on our noses, blurring our vision. What would they give to be so wonderfully young just for this one monsoon? To be so preciously innocent for this once and never again? Who knows where we would be next year or in another ten? Selling in the streets or working government jobs? Married to someone we love or don't? A pirate or a member of the Marxist Party? Living alone or dead? I glance at my sister's lonely, tomboyish face and grin, wet hair sticking onto my forehead like tailored pleat curtains. Mirror images, looking like freedom. The sky is nothing but a seamstress waiting to dress us up in moonlight. A red ant crawls up her eyebrow, and she brushes it aside with her hand. Her hands are delicate summers. The years ahead, working in the fields, will harden them. But not today. Today we're not second-hand children nobody wants to play with, we're fiercely loved. And today, it feels like we're every beautiful thing in the world, every possibility of magic. Like nothing could stop us from being. Like we're worthy of breath. I smile back at her, and we finally sit down, settling into the soaked sand and digging our index fingers into the jackfruit jam. It's 2 a.m. and already tomorrow. Someone once told us that the most dangerous people in the world were those who wanted to live.

I want to live. I want to live. I want to live.

Kochu's Bride-seeing

When the bride walks in,
our mothers talk about her gold.
My brother looks away guiltily
as they tease him.
They share horoscopes.
Discuss auspicious dates.
All this while, he pretends
his dhoti is a skirt.

Raja Ravi Varma

*I'm taking you to the beach right now. I know you're curled
up in a ball on your bathroom floor wondering how to
get past your past or staring at the wall thinking if you
should check up on your ex. Don't. I want you to check up
on you. For the moment, you're with me, your big sister,
okay? We've got our feet buried in the wet sand like two
ostriches sharing a secret with the ground. Beyond the
sea is this magenta-sangria horizon and all these cities
you'll find yourself in, someday. Imagine leaving a bit of
your soul behind in every trek, every airplane, every new
cuisine, like pollen from a rare flower. Imagine, the glory
of having you in all these places. The earth is yours to
romance. Tread on it softly. Don't think of the doors that
shut you in, but of the windows you can look out of. There,
ahead, is this beautiful life I know you deserve to be living.
Not this pile of ash from old lovers' albums. Not this extra
baggage from backstabbers weighing you down. The only
time you should be lying on the floor, tears in your eyes, is
when twenty puppies are licking your face and jumping on
you. From laughing. I'm not saying don't grieve. I'm saying
don't stay there. We romanticize brokenness because when
you're broken you still want to feel beautiful. So you call the
fragments poetry. You call the remains, the cracks of you,
a masterpiece, write fifty poems on how it beats Raja Ravi*

Varma. It's okay. You'll learn along the way that it is not the brokenness that's beautiful, but the bravery. When you're whole again, and I promise you, I promise you that you will be—you will see it was never the brokenness that made you beautiful. The brokenness was beautiful only because you were carrying it. So, let it be gone. Close your eyes and smell saltwater. Somewhere a snail is lugging its home along, somewhere a mother is telling her daughter about mermaids. Think about the books and libraries waiting to meet you. Waiting for the privilege of knowing you. For the pure joy of loving you. Every breath you take is a majestic roar, whether you know it or not. Your life is begging you to live it. If you listen close, you can hear the stars calling you a star. So burn on. Burn on. Burn on.

– For Mol, On the Bad Days

Mattancherry Beef Biryani

We sit around the oil lamp during the power cut,
order beef biryani from Kayees and play a game in the dark:
what is your biggest regret?

'I voted for the wrong party,' my brother says remorsefully.
I voted for the right party, and still we didn't win, I think.

'I kissed someone I didn't love.' *I kissed someone I loved.*
My heart didn't feel so good when he broke up a week later.

'I didn't slap the man who forced himself on me. I wish I had.'
Neither did I. He was my best friend.

'I tried to kill myself,' he says.
My biggest regret is, I'm still alive.

They Laughed at My Braces

When my sister comes home crying after being bullied
   at school,
our grandmother sits us down and makes us both some
   elaichi chai.

What is it now? she asks gently.

'They laughed at my braces.'
*Do you know what they're made of? Steel. The stuff Burj
   Khalifa, the tallest building in the world is made of, she
   says, wiping her tears.*

'They made fun of my spectacles.'
Did you know glass was made by heating sand?
Now everywhere you go, you carry a bit of the beach with you.

'They pick on me because I'm small,' she says.
So was the universe when it started out.

'They said I'll never get anywhere.' Her voice is shaking now.
Our grandmother smiles knowingly.

That's what the shelf told the book.

Beedi

What do you kids want? Baba asks as he steps out. *I'm off
    to the market.*

Maroon lipstick, my sister says.
Beedi, my brother yells from his room.

At night, when everyone's asleep,
they sit across from each other.

How does it look? he asks, pouting.
Fabulous, she says, through the smoke in her mouth.

Off to College

May you be blessed with fantastic makeout sessions and enough cigarettes to get over them. There will be more heartbreaks than relationships, and that's okay. You're off to college in some foreign city and you'll meet a boy who reminds you of fairy lights and handwritten letters. You'll kiss canned beer off the pout of an introverted girl with seafoam green hair at some sorority party and forget about the heteronormative nonsense they teach back here. You'll miss home even though you never loved it. You'll ache for the rosematta rice wrapped in daily Malayalam newspapers, a makeshift substitute for tiffin boxes, and time and again you'll think of eating from the same banana leaf as Mama. You'll even remember that bamboo cane on your teacher's desk fondly and the nuns in the convent who raised you and the mango dripping down your chin and onto the front of your new school uniform. You'll fall in love with your parents only after they're really old and you'll be sad about growing apart from your daredevil sister and your dork of a brother. You'll spill your best secrets to your roommate at 3 a.m. on a Monday you're supposed to be studying for a mock test, and before you know it, the whole class finds out. You'll cry for a week and then you'll be over it, because life is really just that simple, especially when you're that young. You'll be at armed protests and exam halls, boys' washrooms and night clubs, and you'll find

yourself changing in all kinds of ways. Allow that change,
don't mourn it. When you're sobbing into a sweatshirt
some jerk of an ex-boyfriend left behind, think about the
pretty things that still belong to you, like the memory of the
three of us climbing cashew trees and throwing the seedless
fruits at our grandmother for not letting us watch that
Mohanlal movie. Or that one time when we pretended to
have a tummy ache and walked into the nearby chapel and
begged the pastor to give us some wine as medicine. Or our
mother braiding your hair with white ribbons whose ends
were burnt at the tip so they wouldn't come undone. Or
the kajal she made in excitement with sandalwood paste
when she found out you were a girl child. Hold onto the
best of our days. Don't blame yourself for being a gorgeous
Sunday afternoon someone did not want to spend. Your
light is powerful enough to seep through curtains and wake
anyone up, and he's a fool for wanting to stay indoors.
When you fail your first semester, ask your arms to hold
you harder. When every promising friend ghosts you,
invite your coffee machine and poetry books to spend time
with you. When you can't do it anymore, find something
that you can. Wander into university libraries when the
other kids leave you out of their Friday night plans and
fill up your losses with different versions of yourself. The
best thing about falling apart is that you will have the
privilege of experiencing survival. Experiencing growth and
transformation. You're lovely at rock bottom, and lovely

in the sky, but the latter is where you always deserve to be. You deserve flower crowns and mystical landscapes. Baby dolphins and lantern festivals. French kisses and platonic hugs. Everything, everything. So chin up, climb on. Because the world will break you, and you will take your revenge by healing.

—Kochu, before I left for college.

Neil Armstrong

We'd never even seen an airplane, but we wanted to
    be astronauts.

When we pretended to be someone else on days Mama
    and Baba fought, I was Buzz Aldrin so you could be
    Neil Armstrong.

We didn't make it to the moon, Mol. Not even close.
A shuttle accident, you could call it.

Now we meet at family weddings
and you ask me why I don't talk to you anymore.

To say the least, there's no sound
in *empty space*.

A Love Like Mollywood

Body Outlaws

Listen to me, your body is as beautiful as the sky. There's absolutely nothing faulty or second-rate about it. So jump into bed shamelessly, as if every insecurity was just another parachute you didn't need anymore. Make out with that boy you've got the hots for like he's lucky to know the gap in your teeth or the stutter in your voice or your gummy, imperfect smile. If you think you're too short, crane your neck and kiss him tiptoed. Or if you think you're too tall, bend your head and buckle your knees. Ever looked at someone's hands and felt susceptible? Ever heard someone's laugh and felt stripped naked, like that sound was your new mother tongue? Hold onto that feeling. You're never going to see the rain up so close, never going to feel like your bare feet are on soft grass when you run your fingers through his unruly hair, never going to have stars kickboxing your gut as if you were going to vomit glitter. When you want it so bad that you almost unzip each other's skin in a hurry to have your clothes off, you shouldn't agonize over your chipped nails or self-harm scars. When you lie so close to him that your breaths sync, your palms twin, your shoulder blades cut into each other till you bleed sequin, you shouldn't be thinking about your disproportionate arms or grey hair. Or the tiny bulge of your belly or the barrenness of your hips or every damn flaw you tried to finger out. Just make love to him hungrily, mercilessly. Let desperation drip from you like sweat. Get your wild out, let your guard down. Expose yourself unapologetically as if you were the most exquisite thing out there. You are. Touch like your hands have never known calluses. The birthmark on your neck won't matter. The blemish on your chest won't matter. The jiggle on your thighs won't dare matter. You're allowed to smell like forehead kisses and unmade beds. You're allowed to wear your moles and crooked nose and small breasts as if someone held them all night. There's no other way about this. You're never more perfect than right now. You're never going to live like this again. And you're never more beautiful than when you're *feeling* beautiful. Remember that.

Fireflies in a Mason Jar

You were one of those people
who learned heartbreak from their parents,
and it took me exactly two weeks to understand
you were from a broken home.
You sure did look like it.
Broken, I mean.

You wore khadi Nehru jackets and hated fireflies
because that's how your mother
fell for him—how he caught an entire family of them in
a mason jar—and left it near her doorstep.
You were a strange boy.
You once told me the first thing
you learned after your father hit you,
was the number of bones the human body had.
Just to be sure you'd still survive
after the five he snapped
against the waning glow of the lightning bugs.
The second, that
your mother only loved you because you were
the spitting image of him.
I wanted to tell you
if he looked anything like you,
I didn't blame her for loving him.

Last evening, you finally took me to your old town.
We sat at the tea stall where your parents had their first fight,
and watched the fields spark up with things that lit up the dark.
And as the night settled in, you kissed me under a
    flickering street lamp
and all I wanted was to tell you how I hated fireflies too
that I thought mason jars were stupid and God,
I'm so grateful you had two hundred
and one bones left
to survive your father's abuse,
and oh God, yes. *I might love you.*
So much that the two of us sparking up in the middle of a
    ghost town your
parents failed you in, was enough to believe in love again.
So much that I'd burn this wreckage of a town
to give you a better childhood.
So much that the
two of us lighting up,
like twin bonfires left to die with autumn,
was all it took
for a passer-by firefly to think
it was not beautiful
anymore.

Sweet Talker

God's name.
Love poems.
A half-finished beedi. An old flame's
kisses.

Things he wore on his mouth.

But my favourite, was laughter.
And how he smiled at me like
there was something
worth smiling at.

Safe Space

You're the one who excites my demons. You're the one who makes running from them fun. You take my blistered feet and give them ballet dreams. You make my stab wounds look like late-night erotic back rubs. You turn my wars into history museums. You replace my insomnia with pillow talk and moonlight. Come over, extra baggage and all. Come over, because these cigarettes are looking for a mouth and I told them I knew yours. Come over with your neon hair, all your broken, and every single poem you wrote that girl who left. I'll read them. Hell, I'll perform them under the tender glow of the table lamp that kept me awake at sixteen the first time I sedated myself with sleeping pills. We'll turn it into a spotlight for our private show. We'll turn this bed into a matchbox and sleep inside like we never knew we were arsonists. Because I'm so in love with you it's embarrassing. I'm so besotted it's terrifying. And I know you keep saying that I deserve better than your shit, but I want your messed up and I want your ghosts. I want to belong to you in ways I could never belong to myself. I want to make love to you while we hear the sirens of our pasts catching up with us. And I know there are a lot of beautiful places in this world, but your heart is the only safe space I know.
Hide me.

Oru Nadan Crush

i)   Love is not small for me, it is like seismic waves.
     You sent a Richter scale nine point five up my spine
     when you smiled at me the other day.

ii) Your eyes are like gingerbread. Golden-brown
     in sunlight, dark cinnamon at twilight. I keep
     wondering what they look like when you're kissing.

iii) I like the way your mouth moves when you talk
     about your favourite books. The slight curve at the
     edge, a bowstring. The dimple, as if the archer's
     arrow was gently nudging the insides of your cheek.
     Tell me you talk about me too.

iv) Your voice is garden strawberries sunbathing in
     black forest.

v)   The bridge of your nose, an arch. I can rewrite
     history books that don't tell me how white jasmines
     from the Garden of Eden left pollen on your nose
     and with time, they turned into your freckles.

vi) Delicate, the rings under your eyes. I think of
     dreams waiting for you to fall asleep, like giggling
     children. When your eyes close, do they sit on your
     lids and draw those dark circles with colour pencils?

vii) You're magic that's meditating.

viii) You're in my blood like a secret language. You're in all my veins. My pulse is the only poem that reminds me I'm alive.

ix) I want to watch spring turn into summer turn into autumn turn into winter through your eyes. I want tulips and apple cider and sunlight and snow and you.

x) Your smile is a book I want to translate into my mother tongue.

xi) I'll curl up with yellow blankets, neyyappam and cutting chai. I'll read you everyday.

Lullabies

I am convinced that there are mothers who haunt the corridors of government hospitals in their sheer nightgowns, crooning to the miscarried remains of their infants until they fall asleep. I am convinced that there's a comforting melody in the manic giggling of teenage girls who still find their way back home. That every divorce paper ruffled at the right pace whispers sheet music so wretchedly gorgeous it turns a piano somewhere green. That gutted things proud enough to walk on despite the yawning holes in their chests have the most stirring rhythm under their feet. That the last sigh of a ventilator is the most bittersweet soundtrack a corpse will remember for the rest of its death. That if you dig deep enough, ashes inside ancient urns ring with the gratification of this very chorus. It is in every mass mourning. Every therapist's room. Every orphan's handmade Father's Day card. Right from the drone of an ending Sunday night to the lullaby of a childhood photo. That eerie, settled-in melancholy of growing up. The quiet surrender to the fate of losing something, or never having had it in the first place. A peaceful embracing of sorts, that you once lived, and now you must let go. I am convinced that someone can give you this song. That a person can run their whole life from this tune and still have their body hauled back, whistling in ardent denial, in delicious submission. That it is so contagious, all it has to do is play, and you find yourself helplessly humming your way to a tragic downfall. Hamartia, a fatal flaw. What I mean to say is, I'm finally ready. What I mean to say is, there is a price that comes with all this, and I am willing to pay.

You kiss me, and all my bones *sing*.

Lost in Translation

At twilight, we hold hands like it is politically incorrect.
Like we might offend the social Conservatives.
For every apricot sky of mine, you see light scattering.

I like you so much, these days I write poetry on science.
For instance, did you know we get taller in the morning?
You'll have to stay the night to find out if it's true.

Every time I'm home, my mother makes me serve tea
to potential lovers, in a traditional Kerala cotton
saree. Every time you're home, your
neighbourhood aunts keep pushing their pretty
daughters to talk to you.

Talking.
That was always difficult for us, wasn't it?
Your mother tongue is the strangest thing
I don't know how to borrow from
your beautiful, beautiful mouth.

Seerat, you whisper, finger against my cheek. Explain.
Muthu, I say, hands on your chest as you laugh. Explain.

I imagine your brothers yelling:
all these marriageable women in our land

and you chose an outsider?
You imagine my mother crying and beating her chest:
even if he learns our language, he is not one of us.

But I have travelled seas and quicksand to find you.
I have lain empty like a hanger's shoulders till I met you.
I like the differences, I like you.

So what if we get lost in translation?
We've got *love* for subtitles.

Gooseberry Pickle

We loved like we were punishing ourselves.
Like our mouths were exit wounds.

Like our bed could make God masturbate on some days
and call 911 on others.

Urgent hands spilling over each other the way
my mother's Gooseberry pickle did
on my uniform the first day of school.

I still remember walking home crying.
Nothing has changed much.

Vulnerable

I was desperate to belong to you. I was so desperate that I took your indifference and filled it in all the open spaces of my ribs and said, baby, you are the most beautiful thing about my body. If some of you was all I could have, God, I'd take that because I was sick for you. And I know it wrecked me. That someone could be so in love with someone else that they let them vandalize them. You threw rocks at my heart and I still chose you. You abandoned me and I still adored you. Nobody will ever understand how ashamed I was of myself the night you told me you didn't want me anymore. I cried until my lungs felt like loose change. You don't remember because you weren't there to see all that. God, I'm glad you didn't see all that, you'd have been disgusted with me. I know I was. I stayed up the whole night watching the city lights through the rusted window of my 1BHK apartment and punishing myself for not being what you needed.

And you still don't get it. You don't get it at all. I couldn't sleep knowing you were leaving. I spent the whole week smoking and being reckless and demolishing myself. I can still taste the pills in my mouth and the way people in college looked at me the day I overdosed. Or how I passed out for hours only to find my roommate forcing glucose into my mouth and telling me she was so sorry for whatever had happened. I can still feel the bitter medication from the psychiatrist's office stuck in my throat. I was pathetic, and it haunts me. It haunts me that I can't talk about how I almost lost my life that day and you still don't know. That even after I nearly died, I wanted you and I've never felt so miserable and hopeless. It haunts me that the only reason I never told you was because I was terrified you'd never want me back, or worse, regret me, because I've been so stupid.

But after that day, everything's wrong. I can't talk to my grandma the same way when she shakes her head at news articles on teenagers killing themselves and says, kids these days. I can't look my brother in the eye when he asks me why my psychiatrist prescribed drugs to me like I was a goddamn lunatic and told him to supervise the dose. I still remember how his hands shook the first time he gave them to me, like he'd never done this before. I hate that I put him through that. I hate that I spilled my blood for someone like you when all my life I believed my blood was the stuff of revolutions. You, with your Irish coffee eyes and throaty laugh. You, with your freshly mown stubble against my creamy cheek. You, you, you.

If I could, I'd return all the things I don't need anymore.
The paperbacks you bought, but never read.
The cassettes we were two sides of.
That expired gel.
Your old pyjamas.
Our tennis rackets.
But mostly, *myself*.

Come Waltz in My Kitchen

Come waltz in my kitchen
and undress to old ghazals
we'll giggle through port rum
and French kiss our lips
numb
and play our broken hearts
and pretend to grow apart
because who are we kidding?
We only wanted distraction
we were never in love, jaan.
Our demons were just
terrific
dance partners.

Two

Every beautiful thing in the world
came in twos, you said.

A pair of wings.
A pair of earrings.
Lovers.

The first date we went on
we got tangled up in each other
like a pair of shoelaces
never undone.

We were two of *everything*.

Your hand in my hand.
Your leg over my leg.
Your lips on my lips.
Always in twos.

The second time we went out,
your lips came in pairs too-
sometimes, with kisses.
And sometimes, with abuses.

And every time after that
your fists, they were two

my eyes, were seeing double.
Purple, *two*.
Your palms, *two*
Slapping against my cheeks,
two two two

until they were twice the colour they should have been.

It's almost a year since I let you go.
You'd be surprised how far two legs can run.
Or how well a pair of lungs can breathe out toxic things.
And I know you don't understand why I would rather be alone
than be with you, but tonight as I sat in my verandah
staring at my old bruises, I wondered.

Maybe two is not for us, my love.
Maybe two isn't always as beautiful as you think.

After all,
we should've known.

Even handcuffs come in *pairs*.

The Ganges

He tells me I am pure.
So pure you decided to wash your hands off me.
He says he sees streams on my wrists.
*Your body dipped into me like a grieving man trying to
    wipe his sins off.*
He thinks my eyes are clear water.
*Done with me, you looked away, terrified of your own
    reflection.*
He calls my skin a beautiful river.
Finally clean, you leave your scars behind and run.
There is nothing beautiful about carrying scattered ashes.

Damaged Goods

Tell your mother I miss her ginger tea on rainy nights
    with you.

Tell her it's raining again tonight, as I watch it
pour from inside some local bar I stumbled into.

There is no ginger tea here, only other men.
Sometimes, I tell them about you and how you threw
    me away.

And sometimes, they tell me damaged goods
shouldn't have
such kissable lips.

She Was Here

Years from now, you will sit in a Kerala coffee house
with an old lover of mine you met when you were
travelling, and the two of you will joke about me like a
fond memory.

You will tell him, she wrote war poetry and made a big
    deal out of everything, it was exhausting.
And he will tell you, she cried so much I may as well have
    cut the water supply at home.

The two of you will laugh at how I stayed up writing letters
to people who left, and he will say, she was pathetic.
She wasn't the kind of girl a decent boy would bring home.
You will nod your head.

Neither one of you will dare mention that years
after you left, I wrote letters to you too.
That when I ran with the wind, my hair looked like
kite strings reaching out to the wilderness.
You will pretend to forget the smell of my neck,
all mud in the rain, black tea, fresh bread and comfort.
You will pretend to forget the sound of my laughter,
all classic poetry, ancient philosophy.
You will pretend to forget the pine cones I painted in the mist
and the fireflies I chased through fields of paddy

and the way my eyes lit up when I danced with people
     from different cultures
and tried to learn their language and made the raw earth
     my bed.
You will swallow the last of your filter kaapi and ask each
     other what brought you here.
You will both say things like work and food and leisure
     and other lies.
Neither one of you will admit to the other that you still
     hear my heart beat the nights you can't sleep.
That the only souvenir you take back from a new place is
     the guilt of never finding me.
That it kills you to realize I'm the song that grows on you
     after you stop listening to it.
That the only reason you're wandering at all is because
you erased it from the tape and now it's a ghost in your head.
You turned me into a punch line and it wasn't even funny.

And now when you shake his hand and say goodbye,
you stare at it just a second longer. And in the
silence, both your minds echo in
unison: she was here.
She was here.
She was *here*.

Varkala Beach

The first time you kissed me,
I saw my whole life flash before my eyes.

A villa in Varkala beach. Two golden retrievers. Twin coffee
    mugs. Shared blankets. *Love*.

Four years after you walked out
I sit in my lone house by the sea, with my two stray dogs,
    beer bottles littered at my feet
and remember something my grandmother once told me.

There's only once
when your whole life
flashes before your eyes
and it's when you're
dying.

The Woman

You met me on a Monday, by accident.
Just as the men were throwing me out after a bar fight.
You were passing by, and I was reeking of cheap brandy.
I think I saw your jaw drop.

When you asked them who I was, they told you
my name could cut through tongues,
leave them hanging from mouths
like guillotine blades.

I won't lie to you. I was dangerous because
I already knew I was beautiful.
When men on the street ask me why I don't smile,
I tell them they might never *survive* it.

I am laughter so powerful, I can bring cities to their knees.
Hafez and Rumi first discovered poetry
when they pressed their index fingers to my cheeks
and stumbled upon dimples.

I am dangerous because I already know I am brave.
I am dangerous, because when I leave,
I will make you write poetry.

So tell them. Tell them how you still smell burning
frangipanis sifting through your fingers
when you think
about me sighing spring fever into your neck.
How you cycled through the Sea Link lit with golden
    lights
when you traced my spine.
How it felt like skinny-dipping in the Ganges
when you kissed my tears.
I was the bleeding sunset in handcrafted shoes.
I was the Himalayas sitting cross-legged on your couch
wearing ancient runes on my tattooed arms.
I was the realest. Damn. Thing.

Now you don't meet anyone on Mondays, by accident.
You like ordinary Tuesdays and kadak chai and girls who
    laugh like
temple bells. Now you build borders and turn me into a
    national ban.
This is how you recover from my laugh.
This is how you heal.

But you don't tell them about your
recurring nightmares.
The 2.00 a.m. scares when you
wake up in a sweat, screaming a name

that cuts your tongue so bad,
you feel like the French Revolution.
And in your dreams, you see a woman.
A woman dancing to Death Metal
on the roof of an ambulance
like she was afraid of
nothing.

And when she looks straight at you and smiles,
you pick up your heart like an emergency
and *run*.

Sunset

In the evening, the prayers begin.
The men reciting the azan.
The priest performing the aarti.
The bishop reading the Bible.
God pulls out her tampon
and the sky turns *red*.

Letters to Home

Do Not Mistake Me

Do not mistake me for
comfort zones and safe spaces.
For the gentle whirring of the washing
machine and slow dancing in old socks
on a late Thursday evening after work.

Do not mistake me for dried lavender and
incense sticks, scented candles
and '80s mixtapes.
For the comic books and
second-hand paperbacks of
classics and lentil soup served
in floral painted bone china.
I am not any of these beautiful things.

I am hospital bills and unpaid leaves.
I am waiting rooms and mood stabilizers.
Nothing about my body looks like
shared blankets and pillow talk.
My body is a cold bed I want
to wake up from.
I am not your mother's lap.
I am not your ex-lover's shoulder.
I am not your way out of yourself.

Do not mistake me for another
soft thing you can break and
write poetry on,
because I am not that.

I am relaxed ambulances
heading home from the morgue,
with the satisfaction that there
is nothing *left* for you to kill.

Sinking Car

When I come back from therapy
I find Mama waiting in the verandah,
tears cradling her papery lashes.

You could've just talked to me instead, she says.
I look away like a brat who was caught drawing on the walls.
I know she worries for me, but how do you stop a mother
from blaming herself when you tell her that her child is broken?

Would you have understood? I begin softly. She doesn't reply.
I pull out bubble gum to chew out the cutting silence.

Are you in pain? She whispers.
Sometimes.
What does it feel like?
Like I'm trapped in a sinking car.
She furrows her brow,
trying to make sense
of what I just said.
Finally, she asks
full of concern,
are you wearing your seatbelt?

The Pianist

The day I taught my brother and sister to play with marbles, I watched Baba get mad at his mother for using the pages of his sheet music book to spit watermelon seeds onto. When I asked him why she didn't eat them instead, he said she didn't have teeth. The next day, he got a new book and our grandmother begged for him to play. Halfway into his performance, she said, *could you play it louder? I can't hear*.

We burst out laughing, but Baba was red in the face. He swore at her for being deaf, slammed the fallboard shut and vowed he'd never perform for her again. Baba sometimes didn't want our grandmother in the house, but where else could she go? When I asked him why he took care of her, he mumbled things like *obligation* and *returning the favour*.

From then on, we watched her stand outside his locked door, trying to hear all the notes her ears could take. I think she was more proud than curious, but her face had too many wrinkles to tell.

One day, around the time the monsoons began, she was gone. Baba and his brothers sat at her cold feet and talked about arranging her funeral. Under stormy skies, we said goodbye to this tiny old woman in her white saree, and then all our uncles left for different countries the very same day.

In the middle of the night, the song started.

The three of us saw our mother run out of the house in her nightgown, and followed her, panic-stricken. I'll never forget how we eventually found him. How his hands were swollen red from dragging a heavy something.

As our father sat there playing the piano in the cemetery
over and over next to his mother's grave,
his hair damp from the rain,
we watched a man weep
for the first time
but not loud enough.

Not loud enough
for the deaf to hear,
or the *dead*.

Kochu's Lover

His body is your favourite poem.
Nothing could stop you from turning his pages.

When he undresses you, you feel as naked as a
classic novel in the throes of literary analysis.

He has a green thumb. He flicks it across your chest
and water-lilies grow in the starved provinces.

As far as you know, he's everywhere: your thighs.
Your throat. The heavy lids of your eyes.

His bed is a secret library of controversial titles.
His skin, a haiku for coffee monsoons.

Afterwards, you spread yourself on the sofa, eyes closed
and lie there like laissez-faire, allow to do. Anything to you.

You play classical music on his mini brass gramophone
as he begins to put on his Kathakali make-up

and suddenly the two of you are dancing and you're laughing
and you don't care about anything in the world and

for a moment, between his lucid arms, as he twirls
    you around
in a pirouette, you forget how Baba spat paan on your face

and hit you till your cheeks burned, screaming:
boys don't kiss other boys

you shut out the vision of your mother beating her chest
the first time she caught you with the neighbour's son

and the look on your wife's face the day you got married
when you said, *not tonight, I'm sick*

because tonight, you're in love with the ancient language
    of his hips
and how he smells like pressed peacock feathers in a
    Thakazhi book

tonight, you need him like a vulnerable foreigner needs
his passport in a war-oxidized country

tonight, the Heavens are no longer mute spectators:
because when you make love, God utters her first word.

My Mother's English

My mother's English is a dying country.
A jellyfish that has forgotten its sting.
She doesn't know how to say I love you
and that's okay, because neither do I.
Sometimes, she points at the gas stove and tells me, *milk boil*
sometimes she doesn't wake for days and says, *I is sick.*
Once, after school, I found her reading my poems secretly
    and crying.
I swear she translated every word into her native language
with the dictionary in hand.

I asked her if she understood any of them.
She said. *I am pray for you.*

Last week, Baba walked out of the house
and never returned.
My mother's English is a love-hate relationship
with her tongue.
She doesn't know how to say don't leave
and that's okay, because neither do I.

Now there are two things that are broken in this house—
her English and
her heart.

One day, when I got back from school,
I found her burning all my poems in the front yard.
I asked her why and she said, *no more English.*

My mother always said angrezi had
the most *difficult-est* words.
She wasn't too wrong about that.

You see, there's no word for goodbye in our mother tongue,
and my poems
were full of them.

My mother always said
angrezi was a wrong language.
And no matter how many times I asked her why,
she said she just couldn't put *good*
and *bye*
together.

Your Mother's Depression

Your mother is too proud to go to the therapist, so she
    tells you
she will get over this sadness by cooking.
The first month, she lives on Nilgiri tea alone.
The second, her bones begin to show.
You will learn to care for a sick woman the way you learn
    to skip school.
By realizing there is more homework
with every passing day.
You will melt your appetite and feed it to her like Cerelac
    when she tells you she is not hungry,
hunt her demons down and spread their skin over her
    bruises like band-aids.
You will turn her bed into a magic carpet when she can't
    wake up and
press your body against hers like a missing person poster
    on a wall that screams stick-no-bills.
Don't you dare cry.
Not when she does enough of that already.
At fifty-one, your mother feels as empty as a report card
    without a parent's signature.
As useless as a constitution in a fascist country.
And when she does, hold her.
Comb her hair and braid it, and place a jasmine between
    the bobby pins.

Tuck the pleats of her saree and drape the fabric around
    her, left to right just like she dressed you
into your uniform when you were small.
Sing the very lullabies she sang you until morning light
    arrives and she feels beautiful again.
You will watch her whistle to Rafi on the radio as she
    chops the tomatoes.
You will watch her paint her toe nails and head out to the
    temple with coconut offerings
and return with gossip from the local market.
You will tell her she looks younger than you,
and she will blush, her cheeks rich with fuchsia.
At sunset, you will sit on the porch of your verandah,
radiant as ever.
Two women who are back from the dead,
carrying their burning pyres
on their spines.

Fever

Fever, he told himself, his body hot from touch.
Measles, because goosebumps was too pretty a word.
A stomach ache, unless the butterflies proved themselves.
He still remembered the first time Baba called him *sick* for
    loving the neighbour's boy.
What a beautiful way to be ill, he thought.
Of course, he didn't mind dying in bed.

The Art of Metaphors

My mother tells me
if you want to write poetry
you need to master the art of metaphors.
You know. *This is this, and that is that.*

The kitchen sink is not full of her vomit.
The kitchen sink is a *suicide note.*

My mother tells me, everything is a metaphor.
The sky is not blue. The sky is unwashed denim
from Baba's nights out. On its sober days,
it's Neptune bathing in the Pacific.

So I grew up looking at my wrists
and calling them irregular railroads.
There's a blade inside her cabinet that's not
a blade because it's a moving train. My skin
is a track and on its worst days, a coping mechanism.
You, you are not a lover. You're the first novel
I cried over. A Kamala Das poem.
When you look at me, your eyes are not beautiful. Your eyes
are twin skyscrapers watching a city burn
in the early hours of the morning. Sit across from me
on the bed. The bed, that's a lifeboat on overload. If my
mother knew poetry, she'd tell me to be careful

of boys whose smiles were a civil rights violation.
Boys whose hearts were open caskets,
because dead things have the best cases.
What I'm trying to say is,
last evening, I noticed your packed suitcases
and pretended that you had just arrived.

My mother tells me,
I am not a poet until I see how similar
two very different things can be.
A paradox,
and yet, a mirror.

My mother tells me
if you want to write poetry
you need to master the art of metaphors.
I just wish she'd told me how
love is just another
pretty metaphor
for *heartbreak*.

Paper Planes

Our mother only ever loved two things in her life. Us, and
    paper planes. In June,
when the monsoons arrived,
she'd throw them out the window, and watch wistfully.
When I asked her why she had to do this every day, she said
she had to keep the cycle going.

The water cycle? I asked, pointing at my science textbooks,
    but she'd just smile.

The following year, she ran away from us and disappeared.
Baba took us with him and moved to the city, where we
    unpacked
all our things inside a tiny 1 BHK.
What's this? I ask him, pulling out a notebook, its spiral
    bind undone,
almost as if someone had been tearing the pages inside it.
Throw it, he says.

That night, when he's asleep, I sit near the window and
    watch the street lights and lonely skyscrapers.
As I flip through the pages in our mother's notebook,
    I discover poem after poem after poem in her
    handwriting, my heart sinking.

I slowly tear out one page. Fold a poem into a paper plane
and send it out into the horizon.
I imagine a cloud catching it and spreading it open, his
white eyebrows all scrunched up.
I imagine him reading it out loud, his voice a boom box.
Thunder, thunder, thunder. It wakes God up.
God is so moved by our mother's poem, she weeps.

In the morning, when we wake up, the city is all rain.
As we make our way to school, we watch the jasmines bloom.
There is fresh dew on the Ashoka leaves, like scattered words.
The earth is damp from all the things women never say.

I hope *somewhere*, our mother is still writing.

Protest Songs

Call me protest songs in burning cities
call me a mob's victory march before its leader is shot
call me war graffiti from the enemy's blood
but do not call me victim.

Rosary Beads

Today, our mother brings us to church against Baba's wishes. While we take our pew seats, we stare at the pretty boys through eyes half closed in prayer. The ones with snow and berries and freshwater fish for skin. We scan the hallway for the newly married and baptized Mrs Varghese who ran away from her Hindu family, mouthing Jesus songs with equally vigorous fervour as her mother-in-law. Her mother-in-law, who has forest clearings on the plains of her upper lip and calls Kochu, *chakkare*. Sometimes I make Mol cry by telling her she's going to look like her when she grows up. We listen to the mouthy mosquitoes and the grasshopper tripping on the hot candle wax in front of us. Summer has begun and how. Summer, a goddess of plums, flings and group baths in the local temple lake. When the Pastor reads out, *Psalm 34: 18, the Lord is near to the broken-hearted and saves those who are crushed in spirit*, our mother breaks down, the flimsy shawl over her head falling. On days like this, our mother smells like rosary beads and unanswered worship. Old radios and gut-wrenching shame. And then there are days the devil drags her straight into the incendiary chambers of Hell, and she doesn't scream a word, just asks if she can take her hip flask along. When the service is over, the muscles on her face twitch, and her fingers linger on the Bible. *Mama, can we go?* Kochu asks, as everyone begins to leave. *I have homework*. She gets up, dabs at her smeared make-up with the end of her saree, and fixes her face. We walk back home in silence, with the occasional *did you like Varghese Aendy's new beard*? from Mol. *Aunty*, I correct her, rolling my eyes. *That's how you pronounce it, dumbass.* Throughout the bickering, Mama stays solemn. And then Baba opens the door for us, and she breaks into a loud smile, her kajal intact, not a single tear stain on her cheeks, not a single sign of hysteria. Looking into his eyes with the calmness of a woman who knows she's going to the gallows, but still chooses to wear pearls around her neck.

Boxes

Ever since we were kids, we moved cities like the circus,
dropped out of school mid-year and put our toys in
    little boxes.

Today they take me up the treehouse
and ask me if I can keep a secret.

We're shifting again, they say sadly. *We saw it.*
Saw what? *The box. And Mama inside it.*

Spoonerism

Dining room conversations had a habit
of being a simple game in our family
because Baba was a learned man
who loved English more than he loved Mama.

On a Thursday night while passing the bowl of chicken
korma,
a spoon fell from my brother's hand, so Baba picked it up
and said, *have you heard of spoonerism?*
He said it was a slip of the tongue. A play on words. *It's
like swapping the beginning of two words*, he explained.
Shake a tower. Take a shower.
Bad salad. Sad ballad. Bedding wells. Wedding bells.

Our mother hated this game.
You see, Mama didn't know how to read.
Hell, she didn't even know how to speak properly
because they'd married her off to Baba when she was
thirteen. Sometimes she'd call her sister from the
village and talk in broken Hindi, her little body
slumped against the kitchen cabinet.
She'd sit at the table after serving Baba, tight-lipped, tears
streaming down her face.

Soon, my brother and I started talking like this all the
time in school.
Much tea, I told the boy I loved, putting his hands on my
waist. He burst out laughing and said, *you mean,
touch me?*
When the teacher asked my brother to get out of the class
for being noisy, he sneered at her, *bone itch*.
Bone-itch, Bo-nitch. *No, bitch*.

We thought it was our biggest family joke.
Until the night Mama woke us up hours after Baba had
put us to sleep, our bags packed.
She told us we were going back to the village
and when I asked her why, she said, *main padh rahi*.
Hoon, I corrected her. *Main padh rahi hoon*.

After all these years? I asked. *You want to study?*
She shook her head and kept saying, *main padh rahi*.
So we left that night, without Baba, our house burning,
and nothing has ever been the same since.

That night,
I stayed awake
under the dripping roof,
whispering main padh rahi,

trying to make sense of it, rolling the words under my tongue
as fast as I could.

Main padh rahi.
Main-pad-rhi.
Mapedri.
Raped me.